EVER
STOICISM
JOURNAL

A GUIDED WORKBOOK FOR MASTERING SERENITY IN DAILY LIFE

chartwell
books

Quarto

This edition was published in 2024 by Chartwell Books,
an imprint of The Quarto Group
142 West 36th Street, 4th Floor
New York, NY 10018 USA
T (212) 779-4972 F (212) 779-6058
www.Quarto.com

10 9 8 7 6 5 4 3 2 1

ISBN: 978-0-7858-4540-9

Publisher: Wendy Friedman
Senior Publishing Manager: Meredith Mennitt
Editor: Joanne O'Sullivan
Designer: Sue Boylan
Image credits: Shutterstock

Printed in China

CONTENTS

INTRODUCTION

SOMETIME AROUND 300 BCE, a wealthy merchant known as Zeno of Citium was crossing the Mediterranean from Phoenicia to the port of Athens when the ship carrying him wrecked at sea. Miraculously, he survived. This near-death experience hadn't broken him. It had only made him more determined to live his life to the fullest. "Now that I've had a shipwreck, I'm on a good journey," he is reported to have said. "Fortune bids me to be a less encumbered philosopher."

Zeno made his way to the city of Athens. By chance, he came to a book stall where he discovered *Memorabilia* by the Socratic philosopher Xenophon. Zeno was so impressed by the work that he asked the stall owner where the philosophers in town might be found. At that moment, the great Cynic philosopher, Crates, happened to be walking by. Crates took Zeno on as a student.

Zeno studied under some of the most influential philosophers of the day, learning not just the Cynic philosophy, but also the Dialectic method and the philosophy of Plato. Using all that he had learned, he developed his own ideas, which he taught from the Painted Portico or *Stoa Poikile* at the Agora of Athens, the city's main gathering place. His teachings came to be known as Stoicism. Zeno's philosophy offered his followers guidelines for living a wiser, more content and resilient life.

Throughout the millennia since Zeno's life, countless seekers have followed his teachings, from his most famous acolyte, the Roman emperor Marcus Aurelius, to American president Theodore Roosevelt. So how can this ancient philosophy apply to your modern life? You might be surprised how relevant the wisdom of Stoicism is today.

Central to Stoicism is the belief that because we have no control over anything external to ourselves, we must minimize our reactions to those things. It's only through mastering our minds and emotions that contentment can be achieved. Stoics believe adversity isn't something to be avoided. In fact, difficult people and circumstances help us to become better people. Developing good character that will serve you well through any circumstance is among the most important goals of Stoicism.

In this book, you'll encounter the wisdom of the Stoics and discover lessons for your everyday life. You'll find questions that encourage you to reflect on your experiences from a Stoic framework, helping you to shift your perspective and develop a Stoic mindset. With each step on your journey toward developing a Stoic outlook, you'll come to embrace the power of living in the moment and how it can set you free. Through Stoic acceptance, you'll learn to redirect your energy toward the things that really matter to you and achieve a life of contentment and gratitude. Zeno believed that there is no time like the present moment to improve your life. The exercises in this book are a great first step.

WE CANNOT CHOOSE OUR EXTERNAL CIRCUMSTANCES, BUT WE CAN ALWAYS CHOOSE HOW WE RESPOND TO THEM.

EPICTETUS

WHAT IS STOICISM?

If you've heard the word stoic before, you might have a picture in your mind about what it means. Perhaps the word calls to mind a grim-faced person who lives an intentionally tough life devoid of pleasure or who betrays few emotions. There is a common misconception that Stoicism means cutting yourself off from emotions. But that's not what being a Stoic is all about. The goal of Stoics was a virtuous and well-lived life, and they had specific ideas about how to achieve that. They believed that nature contained the divine, so it was perfectly ordered and rational. Therefore, to live a rational life (one in harmony with nature) is to live a virtuous life. Mastering one's own thoughts and feelings is therefore both rational and virtuous.

The Stoics believe that humans are driven by four primary passions or *pathê*, none of which are rational. We feel pleasure at circumstances we judge to be good in the present and desire for those we anticipate will be good in the future. We feel distress at circumstances we judge to be negative in the present and fear those we anticipate will be bad in the future. But really, the Stoics argue, only virtuous circumstances (those in accordance with nature) are truly good. Everything else is neutral and, therefore, our reactions should also be neutral; that is, free of judgment.

FOUR PASSIONS (PATHÊ)

	Present object	Future object
Irrationally judged to be good	Pleasure	Desire
Irrationally judged to be bad	Distress	Fear

Instead of indulging in passions, the Stoics say, we should strive for *apatheia*, or a state of mind undisturbed by passion. While apatheia is the root word for apathy, its connotations are different from what you might think. Instead of not caring about something, apatheia is more about not being bothered by circumstances and being able to maintain serenity and focus regardless of the people or events unfolding around you.

THE FOUR TYPES OF VIRTUE

For the Stoics, the pursuit of virtue is a lifelong effort. It can only be achieved through practice and habits of the mind that must be cultivated continuously. They believed there are four key aspects of virtue:

JUSTICE

According to the Stoics, justice consists of piety, honesty, equity, and fair dealing. In practice, this can be interpreted as treating others with fairness and respect, and aligning our actions with the common good.

WISDOM

Wisdom is required to make logical decisions. The Stoics believe that wisdom is made up of good sense, good calculation, quick-wittedness, discretion, and resourcefulness.

COURAGE

Challenges are used to build character. When we are challenged, our courage is at its strongest.

TEMPERANCE

Temperance in Stoic philosophy is exactly what it sounds like: excess in anything. For the Stoics, it was important to do the right thing, in the right way, consistently, so that it became a habit.

IF YOU ARE PAINED BY EXTERNAL THINGS, IT IS NOT THEY THAT DISTURB YOU, BUT YOUR OWN JUDGMENT OF THEM. AND IT IS IN YOUR POWER TO WIPE OUT THAT JUDGMENT NOW.

MARCUS AURELIUS

THE CORE BELIEFS OF STOICISM

While Stoicism is a deep, extensive school of thought that can take a lifetime to learn, there are a few Stoic principles that are easy to understand.

The goal of Stoicism is to pursue a well-lived life.

Nature is rational, with roles assigned to everything.

The universe is governed by reason. By following the laws of reason, one can achieve harmony with nature.

Difficulty should not be avoided but expected. It provides opportunities to build character.

We can't avoid death, therefore, we should accept it.

External circumstances should not determine our happiness.

We should always examine our reactions to people and circumstances in our lives, and choose our responses.

Intentions are important. We should act intentionally and not irrationally.

Passions are irrational and can't lead us to virtue so they should be avoided. We must pursue a path of moderation and reason.

We can't control anything external to ourselves. We must only focus on what we can control; that is, our own thoughts and feelings.

By focusing on the present and the now, we can avoid some of the worst kinds of suffering: fear of what will happen in the future, for example.

Because everything in nature is connected, we have a duty toward others.

We must accept our fate.

TENETS OF STOICISM FOR MODERN TIMES

From ancient Greek philosopher Zeno to Roman emperor Marcus Aurelius to American philosopher Massimo Pigliucci, thinkers throughout the generations have found ways to apply the tenets of Stoicism. This enduring philosophy has practical applications for our ways of thinking today. We can distill it into practical guidance for everyday life.

LIVE ACCORDING To NATURE

Nature is reasonable and rational. It exists in cycles. Change is a constant. We shouldn't resist change or even death: it's all part of life.

HAPPINESS IS ACHIEVED THROUGH VIRTUOUS LIVING

Material things can't bring us happiness. We can only achieve satisfaction through right living.

WE CAN ONLY CONTROL OUR oWN THOUGHTS AND FEELINGS

Acknowledging that the only things we can control are our own thoughts and feelings has the power to give us serenity.

LET GO OF NEGATIVE THOUGHTS, EMOTIONS, AND PEOPLE WHO DISTRACT US

To be resilient (and therefore conduct a well-lived life), we must let go of egotistical and emotion-driven responses. We can't allow annoyance with others to push us off course.

WE MUST TAKE RESPONSIBILITY FOR OURSELVES

There's no path to happiness, virtue, or wisdom when we outsource our pursuit of them to others. It's only through taking responsibility for our own reactions to the world that we can live virtuously.

WE ALREADY HAVE WHAT WE NEED

There is no external source of virtue or happiness. We are born with what we need inside us. We only need to access and cultivate it.

WE MUST COOPERATE WITH OTHERS

Everyone is interconnected. If we let go of our egos, we can act in accordance with the common good.

STRIVE TO BE BETTER, NOT PERFECT

We can always improve ourselves if we work at it, but we should not set perfection as the goal.

THE STOICS:

HERACLITUS

AROUND 500 BCE

Pre-Stoic Greek Socratic philosopher; inspired the Stoics

SOCRATES

AROUND 470 BCE

Greek philosopher who was a major influence on the Stoics

ZENO OF CITIUM

AROUND 334—262 BCE

Greek Philosopher, considered the Father of Stoicism

CLEANTHES

AROUND 330 BCE—UNKNOWN

Follower of Zeno who became the second leader of the Stoic School of Athens

DIOGENES OF BABYLON

AROUND 230—140 BCE

Greek Philosopher, later leader of the Stoic School of Athens

CHRYSIPPUS

AROUND 279—206 BCE

Student of Cleanthes who became leader of the Stoic School of Athens

THEIR PRECURSORS & FOLLOWERS

CATo THE YoUNGER

AROUND 95—46 BCE

Roman senator and philosopher

GAIUS MUSONIUS RUFUS

25—95 CE

Roman Stoic exiled by Nero

SENECA

AROUND 4 BCE—65 CE

Roman philosopher

EPICTETUS

AROUND 50—135 CE

Greek-born Roman philosopher who was born into slavery

MARCUS AURELIUS

121—180 CE

Roman emperor and philosopher known for his book, *Meditations*

MICHEL DE MONTAIGNE

1533-1592

French philosopher who helped to revive Stoicism

LIVE IN THE PRESENT

BECOMING AWARE of our own thoughts and feelings is an essential part of the Stoic mindset. Those who don't have this kind of awareness are destined to live an unfulfilled life, according to Marcus Aurelius. When we know what we are thinking and feeling, we can also examine our reactions and analyze them, determining what we can and can't control. Once we understand what is within our control, we can begin the process of letting go of our responses toward those things we can't control. Stoicism helps us to transform our negative responses into thoughts that give us a useful perspective on life. That's an important step on the road toward serenity.

In this section, you'll use some of the tools of mindfulness to help you become more aware of your thoughts and feelings to center you in the moment.

YOU COULD LEAVE LIFE RIGHT NOW. LET THAT DETERMINE WHAT YOU DO AND SAY AND THINK. MARCUS AURELIUS

The Stoics had a word for the practice of attention: *prosochê*. It is only by cultivating attention to the present, and to your own thoughts and feelings, that it becomes possible to live a rational and virtuous life.

Mindfulness is a modern practice that can help you to concentrate on feelings, thoughts, or bodily sensations. It can help you to let go of judgment: one of the pillars of Stoicism. Mindfulness helps us to gently observe something with detachment. If you're new to mindfulness, you can start slow. Take a few moments to take stock of your life right now. First, center yourself. Take in the sights, sounds, and smells around you. Observe your breath and the sensations in your body. Now spend a few minutes writing about this moment.

You don't have to be sitting on a cushion to access a meditative state. You can be mindful—paying attention to what's happening in the present—while sitting, walking, cooking, dancing, or even lying in bed. Try this simple exercise to encourage mindfulness. Lay your hands on your lap, palms up or down or if you like, form a circle with your pointer finger and thumb. Set a timer for five to ten minutes.

When you are done with your mindful meditation, try to let go of all thoughts, feelings, and judgment. Simply breathe and notice things. Record your impressions below. Were you able to dismiss intrusive thoughts and keep your focus solely on physical sensations? What kept intruding on your thoughts?

WE LIVE ONLY NOW. EVERYTHING ELSE IS EITHER PASSED OR IS UNKNOWN.

MARCUS AURELIUS

The more you practice paying attention to your thoughts as they occur in the present moment, the more you'll learn about how your mind works. When practicing mindfulness, you want to solely notice and release thoughts. Writing about what those thoughts were later can help you understand what you need to release. What can you do to eliminate negative and distracting thoughts?

CONFINE YoURSELF To THE PRESENT.

MARCUS AURELIUS

Seneca believed that to establish presence of mind for virtuous living, it was necessary to eliminate distractions and preserve one's time and energy. What are some things you are currently giving too much energy and time to that do not better your life? How would you like to change that? What would you eliminate?

Marcus Aurelius believed that it's essential to focus on what matters to you most. If you were limited to only five activities per day (aside from basics like sleeping and eating), what would you do? Make a list below ordered by their importance. Next to each item, explain why it is important to you and what greater goal it helps you to accomplish.

In addition to prioritizing, Marcus Aurelius believed that daily reflection on one's progress was essential. How can you incorporate reflection into your daily Stoic practice?

CONCENTRATE EVERY MINUTE... ON DOING WHAT'S IN FRONT OF YOU WITH PRECISE AND GENUINE SERIOUSNESS, TENDERLY, WILLINGLY, WITH JUSTICE. AND ON FREEING YOURSELF FROM ALL OTHER DISTRACTIONS.

MARCUS AURELIUS

YOU HAVE POWER OVER YOUR MIND — NOT OUTSIDE EVENTS. REALIZE THIS, AND YOU WILL FIND STRENGTH.

MARCUS AURELIUS

What did you do today that helped you to achieve a more virtuous life? What did you do today that was not a good use of your time?

How do your fears and worries about the future distract you from your focus in the present?

What do you think you could achieve if you were able to center yourself in the now instead of allowing your fears to dominate your thoughts?

ZENO OF CITIUM

ZENO was born around 334 BCE in Citium on the island of Cyprus. After a successful career as a merchant, he ended up in Athens and became a student of the Cynic philosopher Crates. Under Crates, he developed his own philosophy and began teaching on the *Stoa Poikile* (Painted Portico). His philosophy came to be known as Stoicism.

Zeno believed that nature (the universe) was rational and, therefore, to live in accordance with nature was to live the best possible life. In order to do so, he taught, we must not be slaves to our passions. Instead, we must develop *apatheia*, a state of detachment and nonjudgment from our thoughts and feelings. We should not wish for a trouble free life, he said, because difficulties help us to build virtue and character.

Zeno's Stoic School of Athens continued after his death, led by those who ascribed to his views. Although none of Zeno's works survived intact, we know of his teachings because of the fragments stated and quoted by those who followed him.

WE HAVE TWO EARS
AND ONE MOUTH,
SO WE SHOULD
LISTEN MORE THAN
WE SAY.

ZENO

EMBRACE DIFFICULTY

IT'S A NATURAL HUMAN INSTINCT to try to avoid pain and suffering. But the Stoics believed that we can attain better character and virtue through enduring difficulty. Every setback is an opportunity to learn, grow, and gain strength. Instead of running from conflict, suffering, and difficulty, we must change both our perspective on a situation and our feelings about it. With a shift in perspective, we can give ourselves both hope and strength.

To learn from our difficulties and discomfort, though, we must understand their source. What is it about this situation that is causing us distress? If we can identify the source, we can change our own response.

In this section of the book, you'll practice identifying the discomfort you feel in challenging situations and reframing it.

NO MAN IS MORE UNHAPPY THAN HE WHO NEVER FACES ADVERSITY. FOR HE IS NOT PERMITTED TO PROVE HIMSELF. SENECA

Think about which aspects of a current difficult situation are in your control and which are not. Use the space below to analyze a situation that's currently causing you stress and pain. How might you shift your perspective so that you can change your reaction to it?

What behaviors have you adopted to avoid suffering or emotional pain? What do you think you have given up in order to protect yourself? What opportunities might you have missed?

If you lived more in the present moment and enjoyed yourself without projecting into the future, what might happen? How would you be a different person if you looked ahead with apatheia, or lack of fear or excessive desire?

FIRE TESTS GOLD,
SUFFERING
TESTS BRAVE MEN.

SENECA

In *Meditations*, Marcus Aurelius wrote: "The impediment to action advances action. What stands in the way becomes the way." What does that expression mean to you? Have you ever turned an obstacle into a new direction? Use the space below to reflect.

THE IMPEDIMENT
To ACTION
ADVANCES ACTION.
WHAT STANDS IN
THE WAY BECOMES
THE WAY.

MARCUS AURELIUS

Use the space below to reframe some of the difficulties you've had as opportunities for growth, learning experiences, and positive experiences that have made you stronger.

CHALLENGES	LEARNINGS & OPPORTUNITES

The Stoics referred to a place inside ourselves called the "inner citadel." This is our retreat and the locus of our strength. It's a place where our distress and obstacles can't reach us. What can you do to build an inner citadel that you can retreat to whenever you need to tap on your own resources?

THE TRUE MAN IS REVEALED IN DIFFICULT TIMES. SO WHEN TROUBLE COMES, THINK OF YOURSELF AS A WRESTLER WHOM GOD, LIKE A TRAINER, HAS PAIRED WITH A TOUGH YOUNG BUCK. FOR WHAT PURPOSE? TO TURN YOU INTO OLYMPIC-CLASS MATERIAL.

EPICTETUS

FOR WE ARE
NATURALLY DISPOSED
To ADMIRE MORE
THAN ANYTHING
ELSE THE MAN WHO
SHoWS FORTITUDE IN
ADVERSITY.

SENECA

Has your anticipation of the future difficulty of a situation or pursuit ever stopped you from doing something? Consider some of the ways that you can stop projecting future outcomes so that they don't prevent you from doing something in the present.

BECAUSE A THING SEEMS DIFFICULT FOR YOU, DO NOT THINK IT IMPOSSIBLE.

MARCUS AURELIUS

The Stoics believed that it is only through mastering our own thoughts and emotions that we can live our best lives. In what ways do you think that your lack of control over your thoughts and emotions is causing difficulty in your life?

DON'T PUT YOUR PURPOSE IN ONE PLACE AND EXPECT TO SEE PROGRESS MADE SOMEWHERE ELSE.

EPICTETUS

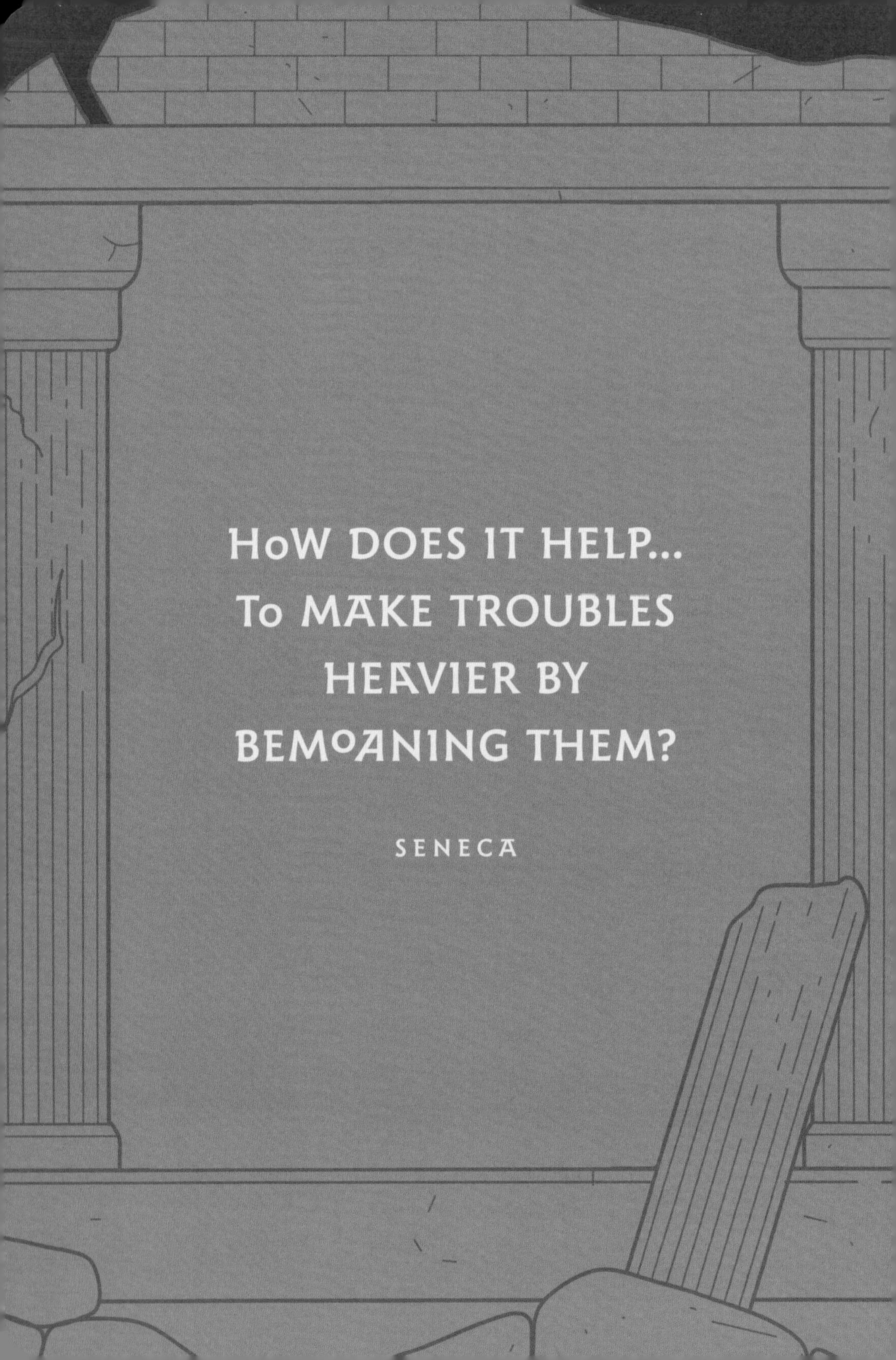

HOW DOES IT HELP...
TO MAKE TROUBLES
HEAVIER BY
BEMOANING THEM?

SENECA

The Stoics believed that if we have enough inner virtue, we can handle any adversity and grow from it. What are you doing on a regular basis to increase your virtue? How can you do more?

STOIC SPOTLIGHT

SENECA

LUCIUS ANNAEUS SENECA was born around 65 BCE in the Roman colony of Corduba, now Cordoba, Spain. He moved to Rome as a young boy and studied oration and philosophy. Due to an illness, he went to live in Egypt with his aunt and uncle. At age 31, he returned to Rome and began his political career. When he ran afoul of the emperor Caligula, he used his philosophical and rhetorical skills to argue his way out of an execution. Instead, he was banished. Later, he was able to return to Rome and served in the senate. He tutored the emperor Nero, who also later tried to have him executed.

Most of his important work was written after he retired. His famous works include *Letters to Lucilius*, and the treatises *On Anger*, *On Mercy*, *On Leisure*, *On the Constancy of the Wise Person*, *On Providence*, and *On Benefits*. He is now considered to have been one of the greatest intellectuals of the Roman empire.

I JUDGE YOU UNFORTUNATE BECAUSE YOU HAVE NEVER LIVED THROUGH MISFORTUNE. YOU HAVE PASSED THROUGH LIFE WITHOUT AN OPPONENT—NO ONE CAN EVER KNOW WHAT YOU ARE CAPABLE OF, NOT EVEN YOU.

SENECA

PRACTICE ACCEPTANCE

BECOMING AWARE of our own thoughts and feelings is an essential part of the Stoic mindset. We can't control external events or circumstances. We can only control our responses to them. In Stoicism, that's called the Dichotomy of Control and it's a way to build our character.

Practicing acceptance builds our emotional resilience. We learn to regulate our emotional responses and train our brains to re-route unproductive thoughts. This will lead to more effective use of our time. Better emotional well-being can also lead to better physical health.

In this section of the book, you'll practice cultivating well-being through acceptance.

YOU HAVE POWER OVER YOUR MIND—NOT OUTSIDE EVENTS. REALIZE THIS, AND YOU WILL FIND STRENGTH. MARCUS AURELIUS

Do you often overreact in stressful situations? In the space below, reflect on a situation in which your thoughts and feelings have led to an overreaction. What do you think you could have done differently?

IF YOU ARE DISTRESSED BY ANYTHING EXTERNAL, THE PAIN IS NOT DUE TO THE THING ITSELF, BUT TO YOUR ESTIMATE OF IT; AND THIS YOU HAVE THE POWER TO REVOKE AT ANY MOMENT.

MARCUS AURELIUS

Does your stress, overthinking, or emotional reactions lead to poor decision-making on your part? Think about a time when detachment could have led you to make better decisions. What could you have done in that moment to better focus on the control of your thoughts and emotions?

When you practice acceptance, you let go of the need to weigh in on every situation with the hope of changing outcomes. After all, it is not rational to believe that you can change every situation. Think of a time when your lack of acceptance to a situation led to frustration and behavior on your part that was counterproductive. What could you have done differently if you had practiced acceptance? How might that have changed the outcome?

YOU ALWAYS OWN THE OPTION OF HAVING NO OPINION. THERE IS NEVER ANY NEED TO GET WORKED UP OR TO TROUBLE YOUR SOUL ABOUT THINGS YOU CAN'T CONTROL. THESE THINGS ARE NOT ASKING TO BE JUDGED BY YOU. LEAVE THEM ALONE.

MARCUS AURELIUS

IT IS THE RESPONSIBILITY OF LEADERSHIP TO WORK INTELLIGENTLY WITH WHAT IS GIVEN, AND NOT WASTE TIME FANTASIZING ABOUT A WORLD OF FLAWLESS PEOPLE AND PERFECT CHOICES.

MARCUS AURELIUS

Part of acceptance means giving up on the idea of perfection. The Stoics believed that we should not let perfect become the enemy of good. What are some of the ways that you irrationally hold on to the idea of perfection? How could you reframe your thoughts to accept the idea that nothing is perfect?

DIFFICULTIES STRENGTHEN THE MIND, AS LABOR DOES THE BODY.

SENECA

Think about an incident from your past that you are holding on to. What is it that makes it hard to let go? What would happen if you looked at it rationally? Would you be able to let it go? Use the space below to work out the situation dispassionately, as if it had happened to someone else. When you are done, consider whether or not you can accept this incident as something that had happened in the past and move on from it.

Are there things about yourself that you'd like to change? List them below on the left side. Then, on the right, consider whether or not these are things that are outside of your control. If they are within your control, how would you change them?

CHALLENGES	LEARNINGS & OPPORTUNITES

In Stoicism, self-love is not about self-care. It's about working toward the virtues of courage, wisdom, temperance and justice. It's about respecting yourself enough to challenge yourself to practice self-control, knowing that it will be beneficial to you in the long run. What are some of the ways you can balance your efforts to achieve virtue through acceptance of yourself?

YOU DON'T LOVE YOURSELF ENOUGH. OR YOU'D LOVE YOUR NATURE TOO, AND WHAT IT DEMANDS OF YOU.

MARCUS AURELIUS

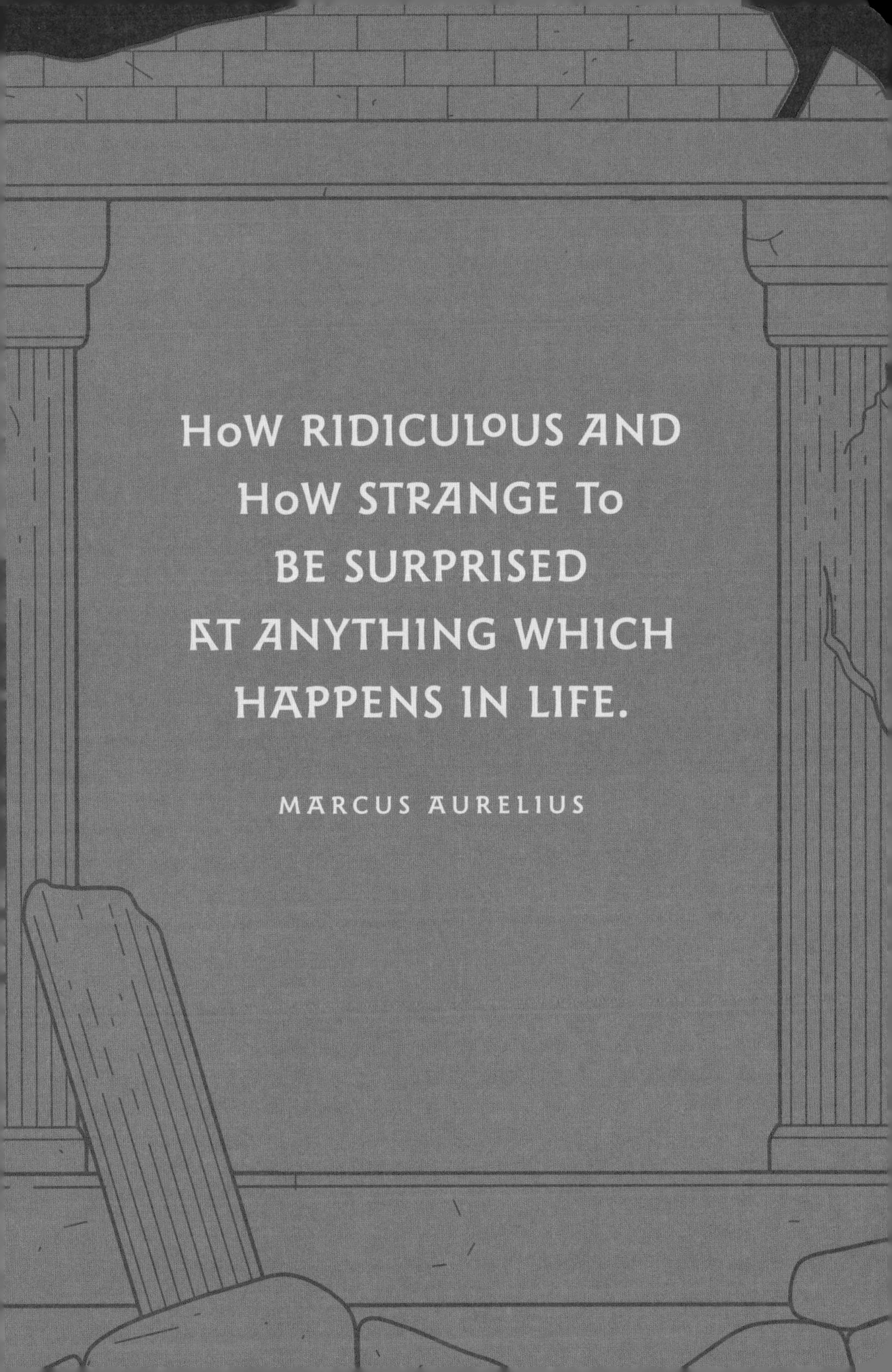

HOW RIDICULOUS AND HOW STRANGE TO BE SURPRISED AT ANYTHING WHICH HAPPENS IN LIFE.

MARCUS AURELIUS

THINK OF ALL THE YEARS PASSED BY IN WHICH YOU SAID TO YOURSELF "I'LL DO IT TOMORROW," AND HOW THE GODS HAVE AGAIN AND AGAIN GRANTED YOU PERIODS OF GRACE OF WHICH YOU HAVE NOT AVAILED YOURSELF. IT IS TIME TO REALIZE THAT YOU ARE A MEMBER OF THE UNIVERSE, THAT YOU ARE BORN OF NATURE ITSELF, AND TO KNOW THAT A LIMIT HAS BEEN SET TO YOUR TIME. USE EVERY MOMENT WISELY, TO PERCEIVE YOUR INNER REFULGENCE, OR 'TWILL BE GONE AND NEVERMORE WITHIN YOUR REACH.

MARCUS AURELIUS

STOIC SPOTLIGHT

MARCUS AURELIUS

MARCUS AURELIUS is considered the most important Stoic. Born into a prominent political family in Rome in 121 CE, he was interested in philosophy from a young age. Two of his tutors were Stoics, and he was especially interested in the *Discourses* of Epictetus, the Greek philosopher and former slave. He entered a life of politics when he was adopted into the imperial family, and in 161 BC was named as co-emperor along with his brother Lucius Verus, who later died in a pandemic.

Although power, wealth, and prestige were of paramount importance in his world, Marcus Aurelius viewed everything through the Stoic framework, so he didn't value these things. He ruled during very turbulent times, and his emphasis on virtue and duty marked his time in power. Although his most famous work, *Meditations*, illustrates the time he devoted to reflection, he also spent most of his time on the battlefield, which is where he died in 180 CE. *Meditations* is one of the key texts of Stoicism, offering wisdom that's been embraced for thousands of years.

A VIRTUOUS LIFE

THE STOICS believed that reason and virtue are key to *eudaimonia*, often translated as "happiness" or "flourishing." True eudaimonia could only be achieved through the practice of virtue, rather than through the pursuit of external achievements. In modern terms, we might say "happiness is an inside job." Virtue is within our power. No matter the external events, individuals can always choose to act virtuously and cultivate moral excellence.

Virtue can only be achieved through resisting those passions that disturb or distress your soul and focusing on what you can control: cultivating courage, wisdom, justice, and temperance, and doing your duty.

In this section of the book, you'll be able to reflect on how you can move toward a more virtuous life.

IF IT IS NOT RIGHT DO NOT DO IT; IF IT IS NOT TRUE DO NOT SAY IT. MARCUS AURELIUS

What does virtue mean to you? How are you currently embodying courage, wisdom, justice, and temperance in your life? In which areas can you do better?

What do you think it would take for you to be a virtuous person and live a virtuous life? Use the space below to express your vision of that. Is there anything stopping you from doing so, starting now?

There are many temptations that lead us away from virtue, all of them from external sources. If we focus on ourselves and what we can control, we can maintain our virtue, even when others around us compromise theirs. What are some things you can do in your work or personal life to be more focused on your own virtue and less on the actions and opinions of others, which might serve to distract you?

ATTACH YOURSELF TO WHAT IS SPIRITUALLY SUPERIOR, REGARDLESS OF WHAT OTHER PEOPLE THINK OR DO. HOLD TO YOUR TRUE ASPIRATIONS NO MATTER WHAT IS GOING ON AROUND YOU.

EPICTETUS

The Stoic emphasis on living in the now challenges us to be our best at every moment. Through our self-discipline and control, we avoid passionate reactions that can cause us and those around us to suffer. Think about a time when you could have benefited from a more rational, less emotional response to a situation. Knowing what you now know about Stoicism, what would you have done differently?

LET EACH THING YOU WOULD DO, SAY, OR INTEND, BE LIKE THAT OF A DYING PERSON.

MARCUS AURELIUS

JUST THAT YOU DO THE RIGHT THING. THE REST DOESN'T MATTER. COLD OR WARM. TIRED OR WELL-RESTED. DESPISED OR HONORED. DYING...OR BUSY WITH OTHER ASSIGNMENTS. BECAUSE DYING, TOO, IS ONE OF OUR ASSIGNMENTS IN LIFE. THERE AS WELL: "TO DO WHAT NEEDS DOING." LOOK INWARD. DON'T LET THE TRUE NATURE OF ANYTHING ELUDE YOU. BEFORE LONG, ALL EXISTING THINGS WILL BE TRANSFORMED, TO RISE LIKE SMOKE (ASSUMING ALL THINGS BECOME ONE) OR BE DISPERSED IN FRAGMENTS...TO MOVE FROM ONE UNSELFISH ACT TO ANOTHER WITH GOD IN MIND. ONLY THERE, DELIGHT AND STILLNESS...WHEN JARRED, UNAVOIDABLY, BY CIRCUMSTANCES, REVERT AT ONCE TO YOURSELF, AND DON'T LOSE THE RHYTHM MORE THAN YOU CAN HELP. YOU'LL HAVE A BETTER GRASP OF THE HARMONY IF YOU KEEP GOING BACK TO IT.

MARCUS AURELIUS

In our achievement and success-oriented world, our benchmarks of success are often external: a first-place trophy, a raise, or a promotion. But the Stoics believed that living a virtuous life was its own reward. How do you pursue virtue, knowing that there is no obvious external reward for it?

NO RANDOM ACTIONS, NONE NOT BASED ON UNDERLYING PRINCIPLES.

MARCUS AURELIUS

The Stoics believed that virtue could be achieved by doing our duty to others. Consider the ways that you might live a better life by giving back, not through money, but through your time and talents. Use the space below to reflect.

FOR WHAT PREVENTS US FROM SAYING THAT THE HAPPY LIFE IS TO HAVE A MIND THAT IS FREE, LOFTY, FEARLESS AND STEADFAST—A MIND THAT IS PLACED BEYOND THE REACH OF FEAR, BEYOND THE REACH OF DESIRE, THAT COUNTS VIRTUE THE ONLY GOOD, BASENESS THE ONLY EVIL, AND ALL ELSE BUT A WORTHLESS MASS OF THINGS, WHICH COME AND GO WITHOUT INCREASING OR DIMINISHING THE HIGHEST GOOD, AND NEITHER SUBTRACT ANY PART FROM THE HAPPY LIFE NOR ADD ANY PART TO IT? A MAN THUS GROUNDED MUST, WHETHER HE WILLS OR NOT, NECESSARILY BE ATTENDED BY CONSTANT CHEERFULNESS AND A JOY THAT IS DEEP AND ISSUES FROM DEEP WITHIN, SINCE HE FINDS DELIGHT IN HIS OWN RESOURCES, AND DESIRES NO JOYS GREATER THAN HIS INNER JOYS.

SENECA

Because you can only control your own thoughts and feelings, it's your own opinion of yourself that really matters, not the opinions of others. Think of a time when you let yourself down. What would you have done differently that would have improved your self-respect? What did you learn from that experience?

NEVER ESTEEM ANYTHING AS OF ADVANTAGE TO YOU THAT WILL MAKE YOU BREAK YOUR WORD OR LOSE YOUR SELF-RESPECT.

MARCUS AURELIUS

In our youth-obsessed culture, the idea of living a longer life is seen as ideal. For the Stoics, though, it was the quality of our lives (and the quality of our souls) that really mattered, not the length. How do you concentrate on building character when so much in our culture seems focused on externals such as youth and beauty?

LIFE IS LIKE A PLAY: IT'S NOT THE LENGTH, BUT THE EXCELLENCE OF THE ACTING THAT MATTERS.

SENECA

WELL, WE SHOULD CHERISH OLD AGE AND ENJOY IT. IT IS FULL OF PLEASURE IF YOU KNOW HOW TO USE IT. FRUIT TASTES MOST DELICIOUS JUST WHEN ITS SEASON IS ENDING.

SENECA

For the Stoics, eudaimonia, or a well-flowing life, involved more than happiness. The word translates to something like "flourishing" with wisdom and virtue. What would a flourishing life look like to you?

What is holding you back from achieving eudaimonia? What steps did you take today to get closer to it?

CLEANTHES

CLEANTHES was born around 330 BCE in Assos, a city in what's now Turkey. He worked as a pugilist (boxer) to support himself financially while studying philosophy. Cleanthes studied under Zeno, the founder of Stoicism, and became one of his most prominent students, taking over from him as the head of the Stoic School in Athens.

Cleanthes is best known for formalizing the Stoic philosophy after Zeno's death. He is credited with numerous works, although few of his original writings have survived. In particular, he is said to have written extensively on Stoic physics and the Stoic concept of the logos (the rational principle governing the universe).

One of Cleanthes' few surviving works is *Hymn to Zeus*, a poetic prayer expressing Stoic beliefs about the nature of the divine and the interconnectedness of all things. This hymn reflects Cleanthes' deep reverence for the rational order of the cosmos and his conviction that human beings should live in harmony with nature.

Cleanthes served as the head of the Stoic School in Athens until his death. He was succeeded by his famous student, Chrysippus, who further developed and expanded Stoic philosophy.

THE WRETCHED, WHOEVER LONG
FOR THE GETTING OF GOOD THINGS,

NEITHER SEE NOR HEAR GOD'S
UNIVERSAL LAW,

BY WHICH, OBEYING WITH UNDERSTANDING,
THEY COULD SHARE IN THE GOOD LIFE.

BUT INSTEAD THEY CHASE AFTER THIS
AND THAT, FAR FROM THE GOOD,

SOME IN THEIR AGGRESSIVE ZEAL FOR FAME,

OTHERS WITH A DISORDERED
OBSESSION WITH PROFITS,

STILL OTHERS IN INDULGENCE AND THE
PLEASURABLE EXERTIONS OF THE BODY.

[THEY DESIRE THE GOOD] BUT
ARE CARRIED OFF HERE AND THERE,

ALL THE WHILE IN ZEALOUS PURSUIT OF
COMPLETELY DIFFERENT OUTCOMES.

CLEANTHES

MASTER YOUR THOUGHTS

OUR RESPONSES TO circumstances out of our control and the behavior of others can cause us to suffer unnecessarily. Our passions or *pathê* lead us to anxiety, fear, or unsatisfied wants. The Stoics believed that if we control our responses and thoughts, we will avoid this kind of suffering and achieve apatheia, or an absence of passions. By focusing on building our own virtues, we won't be distracted by external forces.

In this section, you will begin to examine how you apply judgment to external circumstances and other people, and explore how your life might change if you adopted a more Stoic approach.

YOU BECOME WHAT YOU GIVE YOUR ATTENTION TO. EPICTETUS

What do you currently give your attention to that you know is outside of your control? Have you ever tried to stop thinking about it and let it go? What happens?

PEOPLE ARE NOT DISTURBED BY THINGS, BUT BY THE VIEWS THEY TAKE OF THEM.

EPICTETUS

Does the idea of relinquishing control of all but your own thoughts and feelings make you feel weaker or stronger? Can you imagine feeling liberated if the only thing you needed to control was your own responses to life and the people around you?

IT'S NOT WHAT HAPPENS TO YOU, BUT HOW YOU REACT TO IT THAT MATTERS.

EPICTETUS

Do you spend a lot of time judging people and circumstances? What happens when you change your thinking to a less judgmental approach? Can you think of a time when you withheld judgment? What was the outcome?

REASON SHOWS US THERE IS NOTHING EITHER GOOD OR BAD BUT THINKING MAKES IT SO.

EPICTETUS

We gain better control of our lives when we stop blaming others. What are some of the things that you've blamed others or life's circumstances for that you can let go of in order to live a more Stoic life?

IF WHAT YOU HAVE SEEMS INSUFFICIENT TO YOU, THEN THOUGH YOU POSSESS THE WORLD, YOU WILL YET BE MISERABLE.

SENECA

The need to take charge of others or circumstances outside of our control often stems from fear. What do you think you are really afraid of? How do you think you can overcome that fear?

What external events or circumstances have you allowed to disturb your inner peace today? How can you adopt a more Stoic mindset towards them?

NEVER DEPEND ON THE ADMIRATION OF OTHERS. THERE IS NO STRENGTH IN IT. PERSONAL MERIT CANNOT BE DERIVED FROM AN EXTERNAL SOURCE. IT IS NOT TO BE FOUND IN YOUR PERSONAL ASSOCIATIONS, NOR CAN IT BE FOUND IN THE REGARD OF OTHER PEOPLE. IT IS A FACT OF LIFE THAT OTHER PEOPLE, EVEN PEOPLE WHO LOVE YOU, WILL NOT NECESSARILY AGREE WITH YOUR IDEAS, UNDERSTAND YOU, OR SHARE YOUR ENTHUSIASMS. GROW UP! WHO CARES WHAT OTHER PEOPLE THINK ABOUT YOU!

EPICTETUS

Ego drives us to crave external validation. That can lead to us feeling like we need to control others' opinions of us. How does desiring credit or praise from others disturb your mind? How do you let go of that need and judge yourself only by your internal standards?

THE BEST IDEAS ARE COMMON PROPERTY.

SENECA

Being free of judgment doesn't mean being completely without feeling. The Stoics believed that you should enjoy the beauty and even fun of life. How do you strike a balance between virtue and self-improvement and fun in your life?

IT IS MORE CIVILIZED TO MAKE FUN OF LIFE THAN TO BEWAIL IT.

SENECA

Do you feel at peace with your own thoughts? With your own company? Use the space below to reflect on how you can achieve peace when you allow yourself to let go of judgment, not only of others, but of yourself.

NOTHING, TO MY WAY OF THINKING, IS A BETTER PROOF OF A WELL-ORDERED MIND THAN A MAN'S ABILITY TO STOP JUST WHERE HE IS AND PASS SOME TIME IN HIS OWN COMPANY.

SENECA

You might have heard the expression "Comparison is the thief of joy." While it's not a Stoic expression, it does reflect a Stoic mindset. How can you stop comparing yourself to others? What do you think you would gain if you did?

WHO THEN IS INVINCIBLE? THE ONE WHO CANNOT BE UPSET BY ANYTHING OUTSIDE THEIR REASONED CHOICE.

EPICTETUS

Are your goals rational? What about your responses to the current state of your life? If not, what can you do to set them on a Stoic path?

Think about a current challenge in your life. How can you reframe it as an opportunity to practice a Stoic mindset? Use the space below to write about it.

EPICTETUS

EPICTETUS was born around 55 CE in the city of Hierapolis, located in modern-day Turkey. He grew up as a slave and was taken to Rome to serve Epaphroditus, who formerly served as a slave for emperor Nero. While still a slave, Epictetus had the chance to study philosophy under Musonius Rufus. He later gained his freedom and began to teach Stoicism.

Epictetus' major contribution to Stoicism was around the Dichotomy of Control, which he wrote about in his *Discourses*. This theory asserted that inner peace can only be achieved through understanding and accepting what we can and can't control. He believed that freedom comes from within, through mastery of one's own desires and emotions. In addition to *Discourses*, *Enchiridion* is another of his most famous works. Epictetus influenced all Roman Stoics who came after him, most notably Marcus Aurelius.

HOW LONG ARE YOU GOING TO WAIT BEFORE YOU DEMAND THE BEST FOR YOURSELF AND IN NO INSTANCE BYPASS THE DISCRIMINATIONS OF REASON? YOU HAVE BEEN GIVEN THE PRINCIPLES THAT YOU OUGHT TO ENDORSE, AND YOU HAVE ENDORSED THEM. WHAT KIND OF TEACHER, THEN, ARE YOU STILL WAITING FOR IN ORDER TO REFER YOUR SELF-IMPROVEMENT TO HIM? YOU ARE NO LONGER A BOY, BUT A FULL-GROWN MAN. IF YOU ARE CARELESS AND LAZY NOW AND KEEP PUTTING THINGS OFF AND ALWAYS DEFERRING THE DAY AFTER WHICH YOU WILL ATTEND TO YOURSELF, YOU WILL NOT NOTICE THAT YOU ARE MAKING NO PROGRESS, BUT YOU WILL LIVE AND DIE AS SOMEONE QUITE ORDINARY.

FROM NOW ON, THEN, RESOLVE TO LIVE AS A GROWN-UP WHO IS MAKING PROGRESS, AND MAKE WHATEVER YOU THINK BEST A LAW THAT YOU NEVER SET ASIDE.

EPICTETUS

MASTER YOUR FEELINGS

JUST AS WE MUST LEARN to master our thoughts, we must learn to master our emotions. Feelings such as anger, jealousy, fear and regret distract us from our path to a virtuous life. But it doesn't have to be that way. Our happiness doesn't have to be determined by our response to external circumstances or challenging people and relationships. We can adopt a Stoic mindset and remain serene, non-judgmental, and in harmony with nature.

In this section, we'll look at how we can get the better of our emotions before they get the better of us.

CHOOSE NOT TO BE HARMED, AND YOU WON'T FEEL HARMED. DON'T FEEL HARMED, AND YOU HAVEN'T BEEN. MARCUS AURELIUS

CONCENTRATE EVERY MINUTE LIKE A ROMAN—LIKE A MAN—ON DOING WHAT'S IN FRONT OF YOU WITH PRECISE AND GENUINE SERIOUSNESS, TENDERLY, WILLINGLY, WITH JUSTICE. AND ON FREEING YOURSELF FROM ALL OTHER DISTRACTIONS. YES, YOU CAN—IF YOU DO EVERYTHING AS IF IT WERE THE LAST THING YOU WERE DOING IN YOUR LIFE, AND STOP BEING AIMLESS, STOP LETTING YOUR EMOTIONS OVERRIDE WHAT YOUR MIND TELLS YOU, STOP BEING HYPOCRITICAL, SELF-CENTERED, IRRITABLE. YOU SEE HOW FEW THINGS YOU HAVE TO DO TO LIVE A SATISFYING AND REVERENT LIFE? IF YOU CAN MANAGE THIS, THAT'S ALL EVEN THE GODS CAN ASK OF YOU.

MARCUS AURELIUS

We know that other people's behavior is not something that we can control. Yet it is most frequently the thing that causes us to react, to be disturbed, and to compromise our serenity. What are some ways that you can stop responding to other people's behavior as if you had control over it?

THE KEY IS To KEEP COMPANY ONLY WITH PEOPLE WHO UPLIFT YoU, WHOSE PRESENCE CALLS FORTH YoUR BEST.

EPICTETUS

Does being angry make you feel out of control or in control? Does it feel like a strength or a weakness? How can you make peacefulness a strength?

YOU SHOULDN'T GIVE CIRCUMSTANCES THE POWER TO ROUSE ANGER, FOR THEY DON'T CARE AT ALL.

MARCUS AURELIUS

By striving for apatheia, one can achieve harmony with nature: a state of rationality and logic, undisturbed by the passions of the mind that cause suffering. What can you do today in the service of apatheia—practicing mindful meditation, taking a few moments for reflection and grounding, or journaling? Use the space below to reflect on your progress toward achieving a higher level of apatheia.

FREEDOM IS SECURED NOT BY THE FULFILLING OF MEN'S DESIRES, BUT BY THE REMOVAL OF DESIRE.

EPICTETUS

FRIGHTENED OF CHANGE? BUT WHAT CAN EXIST WITHOUT IT? WHAT'S CLOSER TO NATURE'S HEART? CAN YOU TAKE A HOT BATH AND LEAVE THE FIREWOOD AS IT WAS? EAT FOOD WITHOUT TRANSFORMING IT? CAN ANY VITAL PROCESS TAKE PLACE WITHOUT SOMETHING BEING CHANGED? CAN'T YOU SEE? IT'S JUST THE SAME WITH YOU—AND JUST AS VITAL TO NATURE.

MARCUS AURELIUS

THE HAPPINESS OF THOSE WHO WANT TO BE POPULAR DEPENDS ON OTHERS; THE HAPPINESS OF THOSE WHO SEEK PLEASURE FLUCTUATES WITH MOODS OUTSIDE THEIR CONTROL; BUT THE HAPPINESS OF THE WISE GROWS OUT OF THEIR OWN FREE ACTS.

MARCUS AURELIUS

Think about a time when you wish you'd reacted differently to an emotionally upsetting situation. With what you now know about Stoic philosophy, what do you think you could have done differently? How would it have affected the outcome?

THOSE WHO ARE WELL CONSTITUTED IN THE BODY ENDURE BOTH HEAT AND COLD: AND SO THOSE WHO ARE WELL CONSTITUTED IN THE SOUL ENDURE BOTH ANGER AND GRIEF AND EXCESSIVE JOY AND THE OTHER AFFECTS.

EPICTETUS

The Stoics believed that identifying the root cause of something that's causing emotional distress could lead one to develop a more rational response to it. Think of an issue that's been troubling you. Use the space below to explore what the root cause might be.

Once you have identified the root cause of a troubling emotion, you have knowledge that will help you to let go of your passion or the disturbance around it. Looking at the source you identified, how could you respond to it in a rational rather than emotional way?

If we can speak without undue emotion, our messages and intention can be more clearly heard. What are some things you have tried that makes your speech more rational and less emotional? Can you see a difference in the outcome when you adopt a less emotional response for communication?

LET US SAY WHAT WE FEEL AND FEEL WHAT WE SAY; LET SPEECH HARMONIZE WITH LIFE.

SENECA

WHO DOES NOT ADMIT THAT ALL THE EMOTIONS FLOW AS IT WERE FROM A CERTAIN NATURAL SOURCE? WE ARE ENDOWED BY NATURE WITH AN INTEREST IN OUR OWN WELL-BEING; BUT THIS VERY INTEREST, WHEN OVERINDULGED, BECOMES A VICE. NATURE HAS INTERMINGLED PLEASURE WITH NECESSARY THINGS—NOT IN ORDER THAT WE SHOULD SEEK PLEASURE, BUT IN ORDER THAT THE ADDITION OF PLEASURE MAY MAKE THE INDISPENSABLE MEANS OF EXISTENCE ATTRACTIVE TO OUR EYES. SHOULD IT CLAIM RIGHTS OF ITS OWN, IT IS LUXURY. LET US THEREFORE RESIST THESE FAULTS WHEN THEY ARE DEMANDING ENTRANCE, BECAUSE, AS I HAVE SAID, IT IS EASIER TO DENY THEM ADMITTANCE THAN TO MAKE THEM DEPART.

EPICTETUS

STOIC SPOTLIGHT

GAIUS MUSONIUS RUFUS

BORN AROUND 30 CE in Volsinii, a Roman city located in what's now the Italian city of Orvieto, Gaius Musonius Rufus became known as a great Stoic teacher. He didn't limit his teaching to men, which was quite revolutionary at the time. His most famous student was Epictetus.

Musonius Rufus was known for his commitment to virtue and to a simple life, including eating a vegetarian diet, maintaining one's physical health, dressing simply, and eschewing luxury. He believed that an austere lifestyle prepared people for the inevitable hardships that life presents. He stressed marital fidelity and stability in relationships. He advocated for large families, believing this was in accordance with nature. In his rhetorical style, he emphasized not showing off or trying to appear clever, but centering on virtue.

Only a few of his quotes and longer discourses have survived, but they are frequently referenced by other philosophers who were his students or who were inspired by him.

TO ACCEPT INJURY WITHOUT A SPIRIT OF SAVAGE RESENTMENT—TO SHOW OURSELVES MERCIFUL TOWARD THOSE WHO WRONG US—BEING A SOURCE OF GOOD HOPE TO THEM—IS CHARACTERISTIC OF A BENEVOLENT AND CIVILIZED WAY OF LIFE.

MUSONIUS RUFUS

LIVE IN GRATITUDE

To THE SToICS, the knowledge that life is brief and temporary makes it incumbent upon us to make the most of it and not waste any time on useless thoughts and emotions. When we embrace gratitude, we are less likely to get caught up in negativity and can focus our actions on achieving virtue.

In this section, we'll work toward building our inner resources of gratitude.

WHEN YoU ARISE IN THE MORNING, THINK OF WHAT A PRECIOUS PRIVILEGE IT IS To BE ALIVE—To BREATHE, To THINK, To ENJoY, To LOVE. MARCUS AURELIUS

What are you grateful for now in your life? Use the space below to reflect.

The Stoics believed that nature contained the divine, therefore it was perfect. Spending time in nature and being in harmony with it was essential for them. How do you express your gratitude for nature? Use the space below.

DWELL ON THE BEAUTY OF LIFE. WATCH THE STARS AND SEE YOURSELF RUNNING WITH THEM.

MARCUS AURELIUS

AT DAWN, WHEN YOU HAVE TROUBLE GETTING OUT OF BED, TELL YOURSELF: "I HAVE TO GO TO WORK—AS A HUMAN BEING. WHAT DO I HAVE TO COMPLAIN OF, IF I'M GOING TO DO WHAT I WAS BORN FOR—THE THINGS I WAS BROUGHT INTO THE WORLD TO DO? OR IS THIS WHAT I WAS CREATED FOR? TO HUDDLE UNDER THE BLANKETS AND STAY WARM?"

MARCUS AURELIUS

To approach life with purpose and gratitude allows us to strengthen all of our virtues. How does gratitude give you more knowledge, courage, and temperance, and help you to better pursue justice?

NOTHING IS MORE HONORABLE THAN A GRATEFUL HEART.

SENECA

DO NOT INDULGE IN DREAMS OF HAVING WHAT YOU HAVE NOT, BUT RECKON UPON THE CHIEF OF THE BLESSINGS YOU DO POSSESS, AND THEN THANKFULLY REMEMBER HOW YOU WOULD CRAVE FOR THEM IF THEY WERE NOT YOURS.

MARCUS AURELIUS

SO YOU WERE BORN TO FEEL "NICE"? INSTEAD OF DOING THINGS AND EXPERIENCING THEM? DON'T YOU SEE THE PLANTS, THE BIRDS, THE ANTS AND SPIDERS AND BEES GOING ABOUT THEIR INDIVIDUAL TASKS, PUTTING THE WORLD IN ORDER, AS BEST THEY CAN? AND YOU'RE NOT WILLING TO DO YOUR JOB AS A HUMAN BEING? WHY AREN'T YOU RUNNING TO DO WHAT YOUR NATURE DEMANDS?

MARCUS AURELIUS

We must be grateful for all life brings us: the good and the challenging. How is avoiding discomfort preventing you from becoming wiser and more virtuous? What would a more rational approach to discomfort look like?

Knowing that life is temporary gives us a renewed appreciation for it. How are you working toward making the most of each day?

WHILE THE FATES PERMIT, LIVE HAPPILY; LIFE SPEEDS ON WITH HURRIED STEP, AND WITH WINGED DAYS THE WHEEL OF THE HEADLONG YEAR IS TURNED.

SENECA

Doing service for others is a Stoic ideal. It not only helps us fulfill our duty, but also makes us grateful for what we have. Use the space below to reflect on how using your skills and virtue in service of the common good helps you to cultivate gratitude for what you've got.

MAN IS BORN FOR DEEDS OF KINDNESS.

MARCUS AURELIUS

Gratitude and serenity are linked for the Stoics. If we adopt an attitude of gratitude, we will naturally feel more content. Use the space below to reflect on how feeling grateful affects your outlook on life.

STAY CALM AND SERENE REGARDLESS OF WHAT LIFE THROWS AT YOU.

MARCUS AURELIUS

ALL YOU NEED ARE THESE: CERTAINTY OF JUDGMENT IN THE PRESENT MOMENT; ACTION FOR THE COMMON GOOD IN THE PRESENT MOMENT; AND AN ATTITUDE OF GRATITUDE IN THE PRESENT MOMENT FOR ANYTHING THAT COMES YOUR WAY.

MARCUS AURELIUS

EVERY HABIT AND FACULTY IS CONFIRMED AND STRENGTHENED BY THE CORRESPONDING ACTIONS, THAT OF WALKING BY WALKING, THAT OF RUNNING BY RUNNING. IF YOU WISH TO BE A GOOD READER, READ; IF YOU WISH TO BE A GOOD WRITER, WRITE. IF YOU SHOULD GIVE UP READING FOR THIRTY DAYS ONE AFTER THE OTHER, AND BE ENGAGED IN SOMETHING ELSE, YOU WILL KNOW WHAT HAPPENS. SO ALSO IF YOU LIE IN BED FOR TEN DAYS, GET UP AND TRY TO TAKE A RATHER LONG WALK, AND YOU WILL SEE HOW WOBBLY YOUR LEGS ARE. IN GENERAL, THEREFORE, IF YOU WANT TO DO SOMETHING, MAKE A HABIT OF IT; IF YOU WANT NOT TO DO SOMETHING, REFRAIN FROM DOING IT, AND ACCUSTOM YOURSELF TO SOMETHING ELSE INSTEAD.

EPICTETUS

Marcus Aurelius believed that daily reflection on one's progress toward a more virtuous life was essential. How can you incorporate reflection into your daily Stoic habits?

STOIC SPOTLIGHT

DIOGENES OF BABYLON

DIOGENES of Babylon was born in the city of Seleucia, in what's now Iraq, around 240 BCE. While it's not clear when he arrived in Athens, he studied there under Chrysippus, whom he later succeeded as the leader of the Stoic School.

Although much of his writings have been lost through time, he was prolific on the topics of ethics, natural philosophy, and logic. Stoicism emphasizes the importance of virtue as the highest good and the key to a eudaimonic (flourishing) life. He believed that living in accordance with nature and cultivating virtue were essential for achieving serenity. He is best known for *Dialectic Art*, *On the Ruling Faculty of the Soul*, *On Music* and *On Rhetoric*.

Diogenes of Babylon died around 150 BCE. It's said that his visit to Rome helped to popularize Stoicism in the Roman empire.

NO MAN IS HURT BUT BY HIMSELF. ...LITERALLY, BY HOW HE INTERPRETS WHAT HAPPENS TO HIM. IF HE FOCUSES ON HOW IT COULD HAVE BEEN BETTER, HE WILL BE HURT. IF HE FOCUSES ON HOW IT COULD HAVE BEEN WORSE, HE WILL BE HAPPY. THE *SAME* IS TRUE FOR WOMEN, TOO.

DIOGENES OF BABYLON

ACCEPT YOUR FATE

THE STOICS BELIEVED that pushing against what life gives you is a waste of time. Instead, you should embrace everything that life throws your way. In this way, there are no misfortunes, only opportunities for growth. There are no difficult people, only possibilities to express your character. Reflect on where you are on your journey for this aspect of Stoicism. Have you made progress toward acceptance?

In this section, we'll look at ways you can strengthen your virtue so that you can accept whatever life sends your way.

ACCEPT THE THINGS TO WHICH FATE BINDS YOU, AND LOVE THE PEOPLE WITH WHOM FATE BRINGS YOU TOGETHER, BUT DO SO WITH ALL YOUR HEART. MARCUS AURELIUS

The Stoics believed in accepting fate, but that didn't mean falling victim to it. When something bad happened to you, they believed you could turn it into both an opportunity to improve your character and take a new direction. Look at a challenge that you have faced or are now facing. How can it serve your quest for a more virtuous life?

ON THE OCCASION OF EVERY ACCIDENT THAT BEFALLS YOU, REMEMBER TO TURN TO YOURSELF AND INQUIRE WHAT POWER YOU HAVE FOR TURNING IT TO USE.

EPICTETUS

Cleanthes wrote: "The willing are led by fate, the reluctant are dragged." What do you think he meant by that? How would accepting your fate (and not resisting it) lead you to a more peaceful life?

THE WILLING ARE LED BY FATE, THE RELUCTANT ARE DRAGGED.

CLEANTHES

HERE IS YOUR GREAT SOUL—
THE MAN WHO HAS GIVEN
HIMSELF OVER TO FATE;
ON THE OTHER HAND,
THAT MAN IS A WEAKLING
AND A DEGENERATE WHO
STRUGGLES AND MALIGNS
THE ORDER OF THE UNIVERSE
AND WOULD RATHER
REFORM THE GODS THAN
REFORM HIMSELF.

SENECA

The Stoics believed that focus on having a long life detracts from our efforts to have a good one. What are you now doing to make sure you are making the most of every day in terms of your virtue?

GIVE ME BY ALL MEANS THE SHORTER AND NOBLER LIFE, INSTEAD OF ONE THAT IS LONGER BUT OF LESS ACCOUNT!

EPICTETUS

How would your life change if you loved everything that happened to you, rather than resenting or bemoaning it? What would you need to do to make this shift?

To LOVE ONLY WHAT HAPPENS, WHAT WAS DESTINED. NO GREATER HARMONY.

EPICTETUS

How have you come to terms with the fact that life is temporary? What are some of the ways you can accept the natural process of aging with grace?

GROWING OLD IS NOT SO BAD WHEN YOU CONSIDER THE ALTERNATIVE.

CATO THE YOUNGER

FATE IS A SEMPITERNAL AND UNCHANGEABLE SERIES AND CHAIN OF THINGS, ROLLING AND UNRAVELING ITSELF THROUGH ETERNAL SEQUENCES OF CAUSE AND EFFECT, OF WHICH IT IS COMPOSED AND COMPOUNDED.

CHRYSIPPUS

Because acceptance of death is part of acceptance of fate, the Stoics believed it was imperative that we appreciate the life that is given to us in each moment rather than hoping for more. Use the space below to express gratitude for your life.

NO MAN CAN HAVE A PEACEFUL LIFE WHO THINKS Too MUCH ABOUT LENGTHENING IT.

SENECA

Each day is a gift, according to the Stoics. So, when we are given another one, we should rejoice and not take it for granted. What did you do today to appreciate the gift of another day? What will you do tomorrow if you are lucky enough to receive this gift again?

THINK OF THE LIFE YOU HAVE LIVED UNTIL NOW AS OVER AND, AS A DEAD MAN, SEE WHAT'S LEFT AS A BONUS AND LIVE IT ACCORDING TO NATURE. LOVE THE HAND THAT FATE DEALS YOU AND PLAY IT AS YOUR OWN, FOR WHAT COULD BE MORE FITTING?

MARCUS AURELIUS

Do not waste what remains of your life in speculating about your neighbors, unless with a view to some mutual benefit. To wonder what so-and-so is doing and why, or what he is saying, or thinking, or scheming—in a word, anything that distracts you from fidelity to the ruler within you—means a loss of opportunity for some other task.

Marcus Aurelius

STOIC SPOTLIGHT

HERACLITUS

HERACLITUS is believed to have been born around 500 BCE in Ephesus, a city in what is now modern-day Turkey. Most of what we know about his life and work comes from references made by other philosophers. It's believed that he was born into a wealthy family but gave up his belongings to pursue a life of solitude and contemplation.

Heraclitus is best known for his doctrine of change, exemplified in one of his most famous quotes: "You cannot step into the same river twice, for fresh waters are ever flowing in upon you." This reflected his belief that the universe is in a constant state of flux, and that change is fundamental to existence. He's also known for the concept of the "unity of opposites": the belief that opposing forces are interconnected and necessary for the harmony and balance of the cosmos.

Although only fragments of his work survived, it had a significant influence on the philosophers who came after him including Plato, Aristotle, Hegel, and Nietzsche.

GOOD CHARACTER IS NOT FORMED IN A WEEK OR A MONTH. IT IS CREATED LITTLE BY LITTLE, DAY BY DAY. PROTRACTED AND PATIENT EFFORT IS NEEDED TO DEVELOP GOOD CHARACTER.

HERACLITUS

CHOOSE SERENITY

WHEN YOU FOCUS both on what you can control (your own thoughts, feelings, and actions) and on living in the present, you'll find an amazing transformation takes place: you achieve peace. According to the Stoics, we are not necessarily born with this peace: it is something we learn to cultivate through practice. This peace is within your reach if you are willing to put in the work.

In this section, we'll focus on how you can strengthen your inner peace, an essential element for achieving a flourishing life.

CURB YOUR DESIRE—DON'T SET YOUR HEART ON SO MANY THINGS AND YOU WILL GET WHAT YOU NEED. EPICTETUS

Marcus Aurelius believed that building time into each day for reflection was essential for peace of mind. Do you give yourself enough time for reflection each day? What do you notice if you don't take that time?

Seneca's *Of Peace of Mind* is a response to his friend's request for advice. In the book, he asserts that peace of mind is the greatest goal to aspire toward. But how do you achieve it? One of the things that plagues people the most is inertia: the inability to change. Do you suffer from inertia? What are some of the things you need to do to break this cycle?

THERE IS ONLY ONE WAY TO HAPPINESS AND THAT IS TO CEASE WORRYING ABOUT THINGS WHICH ARE BEYOND THE POWER OF OUR WILL.

EPICTETUS

Epictetus believed that we have everything we need to be peaceful and resilient inside us. Use the space below to take an inventory of your inner resources.

REMEMBER THAT FOR EVERY CHALLENGE YOU FACE, YOU HAVE THE RESOURCES WITHIN YOU TO COPE WITH THAT CHALLENGE. IF YOU ARE INAPPROPRIATELY ATTRACTED TO SOMEONE, YOU WILL FIND YOU HAVE THE RESOURCE OF SELF-RESTRAINT. WHEN YOU HAVE PAIN, YOU HAVE THE RESOURCE OF ENDURANCE. WHEN YOU ARE INSULTED, YOU HAVE THE RESOURCE OF PATIENCE. IF YOU START THINKING ALONG THESE LINES, SOON YOU WILL FIND THAT YOU DON'T HAVE A SINGLE CHALLENGE FOR WHICH YOU DON'T HAVE THE RESOURCE TO COPE.

MARCUS AURELIUS

Our inner resources are like a toolbox that we can use to fix problems that arise in our lives. Now that you've done an inventory of them, which tools do you rely on the most? Which ones have you neglected reaching for and could develop more?

Have you ever heard the expression "Don't run from your problems"? The implication is that taking yourself to a new place will not solve your difficulties. You must learn to address them yourself. How do you confront what's difficult for you?

IF YOU REALLY WANT TO ESCAPE THE THINGS THAT HARASS YOU, WHAT YOU'RE NEEDING IS NOT TO BE IN A DIFFERENT PLACE BUT TO BE A DIFFERENT PERSON.

EPICTETUS

Other peoples' opinions of us are not within our control. And yet, we allow them to disturb our peace. Marcus Aurelius said that if our actions are virtuous, what other people think of us is not our concern. What can you do to worry less about what other people think of you?

IF ANY MAN DESPISES ME, THAT IS HIS PROBLEM. MY ONLY CONCERN IS NOT DOING OR SAYING ANYTHING DESERVING OF CONTEMPT.

MARCUS AURELIUS

One clear way to forfeit our peace is to worry about things before they happen. How do you avoid catastrophizing and live in the present instead?

MAN IS NOT WORRIED BY REAL PROBLEMS SO MUCH AS BY HIS IMAGINED ANXIETIES ABOUT REAL PROBLEMS.

EPICTETUS

By letting go of your attachment to a specific outcome, you will bring yourself peace and accept your fate. What desired outcomes can you begin to let go of today?

PEOPLE LOOK FOR RETREATS FOR THEMSELVES, IN THE COUNTRY, BY THE COAST, OR IN THE HILLS. THERE IS NOWHERE THAT A PERSON CAN FIND A MORE PEACEFUL AND TROUBLE-FREE RETREAT THAN IN HIS OWN MIND. . . . SO CONSTANTLY GIVE YOURSELF THIS RETREAT AND RENEW YOURSELF.

MARCUS AURELIUS

What are you afraid will happen if you let go of external expectations? Is that fear rational?

IS YOUR CUCUMBER BITTER? THROW IT AWAY. ARE THERE BRIARS IN YOUR PATH? TURN ASIDE. THAT IS ENOUGH. DO NOT GO ON AND SAY, "WHY WERE THINGS OF THIS SORT EVER BROUGHT INTO THIS WORLD?" NEITHER INTOLERABLE NOR EVERLASTING—IF THOU BEAREST IN MIND THAT IT HAS ITS LIMITS, AND IF THOU ADDEST NOTHING TO IT IN IMAGINATION. PAIN IS EITHER AN EVIL TO THE BODY (THEN LET THE BODY SAY WHAT IT THINKS OF IT!)—OR TO THE SOUL. BUT IT IS IN THE POWER OF THE SOUL TO MAINTAIN ITS OWN SERENITY AND TRANQUILITY. . .

MARCUS AURELIUS

CATO THE YOUNGER

CATO THE YOUNGER, also known as Marcus Porcius Cato, was born into a wealthy Roman family in 95 BCE. Growing up, he was educated in philosophy and studied the Stoics, but ended up entering politics instead. He held many bureaucratic and political roles before eventually reaching the rank of senator. Throughout his career, he was a champion of the common people. He helped create a public library. But he made himself an enemy of Julius Caesar, of whom he was openly critical.

Cato was a fierce defender of Roman traditions. He was known for his Spartan lifestyle: he walked everywhere instead of riding, was often barefoot, and wore a simple toga. He believed his choices to be symbolic of Roman virtue. When his feud with Caesar escalated, he was forced to leave the Empire and ultimately fled to what's now North Africa.

Cato is known primarily for writing *Origins*, which is about the history of Rome and *On Farming*. Most of what we know about him comes from his contemporaries or writers who sought to memorialize him.

AN ANGRY MAN OPENS HIS MOUTH AND SHUTS HIS EYES.

CATO THE YOUNGER

CULTIVATE WISDOM

WISDOM IS ONE of the four virtues of Stoicism. The word philosophy itself means "love of wisdom." For the Stoics, wisdom meant knowing what is good, what is evil, and what is neither good nor evil; what to choose, not to choose, and what is indifferent.

Wisdom is not something that we are born with, but something we must constantly strive to cultivate.

In this section, we'll look at ways you can focus on building your inner resource of wisdom.

KNOW, FIRST WHO YOU ARE, AND THEN ADORN YOURSELF ACCORDINGLY. EPICTETUS

The Stoics believed that we must think before we speak. Essentially, they believed if we don't have something wise to say, we shouldn't say anything at all. How do you discipline yourself to keep from speaking when what you have to say is more opinion than truth or is informed by emotion, not reason?

EVERYONE HAS THE GIFT OF SPEECH. BUT FEW HAVE THE GIFT OF WISDOM.

CATO THE YOUNGER

To gain wisdom, we must be willing to learn and adopt a beginner's mindset. Does putting yourself in the position of a learner feel challenging to you? What do you need to give up in order to be open to learn?

IF YOU WANT TO IMPROVE, BE CONTENT TO BE THOUGHT FOOLISH AND STUPID.

EPICTETUS

WERE YOU TO LIVE THREE THOUSAND YEARS, OR EVEN THIRTY THOUSAND, REMEMBER THAT THE SOLE LIFE WHICH A MAN CAN LOSE IS THAT WHICH HE IS LIVING AT THE MOMENT; AND FURTHERMORE, THAT HE CAN HAVE NO OTHER LIFE EXCEPT THE ONE HE LOSES.

MARCUS AURELIUS

If we are open to learning, we can observe and learn from our own mistakes and those of others. What are some lessons you've learned from your mistakes or the mistakes of those around you? How did these mistakes help redirect you?

WISE MEN ARE MORE DEPENDENT ON FOOLS THAN FOOLS ARE ON WISE MEN.

CATO THE YOUNGER

When it comes to knowledge, the Stoics had a 'garbage in, garbage out' perspective; that is, you must be discerning when it comes to your source of information and ensure that the 'wisdom' you receive is truly wise. How do you vet your sources of information? How do you ensure that you are taking in the best quality information that emphasizes truth?

IT DOES NOT MATTER HOW MANY BOOKS YOU HAVE, BUT HOW GOOD THE BOOKS ARE WHICH YOU HAVE.

SENECA

Sometimes we can get caught up in projecting the appearance of wisdom, rather than focusing on true wisdom, which doesn't need to be acknowledged by others. What egoistic needs do you need to let you of in order to achieve true wisdom, not just its appearance?

DO NOT TRY TO SEEM WISE TO OTHERS. IF YOU WANT TO LIVE A WISE LIFE, LIVE IT ON YOUR OWN TERMS AND IN YOUR OWN EYES.

EPICTETUS

DON'T JUST SAY YOU HAVE READ BOOKS. SHOW THAT THROUGH THEM YOU HAVE LEARNED TO THINK BETTER, TO BE A MORE DISCRIMINATING AND REFLECTIVE PERSON. BOOKS ARE THE TRAINING WEIGHTS OF THE MIND. THEY ARE VERY HELPFUL, BUT IT WOULD BE A BAD MISTAKE TO SUPPOSE THAT ONE HAS MADE PROGRESS SIMPLY BY HAVING INTERNALIZED THEIR CONTENTS.

EPICTETUS

When we begin to think we know it all, we stop learning. How do you keep your mind open to receiving new wisdom?

IT IS IMPOSSIBLE FOR A MAN TO LEARN WHAT HE THINKS HE ALREADY KNOWS.

EPICTETUS

IF SOMEONE IS ABLE TO SHOW ME THAT WHAT I THINK OR DO IS NOT RIGHT, I WILL HAPPILY CHANGE, FOR I SEEK THE TRUTH, BY WHICH NO ONE WAS EVER TRULY HARMED. IT IS THE PERSON WHO CONTINUES IN HIS SELF-DECEPTION AND IGNORANCE WHO IS HARMED.

MARCUS AURELIUS

The Stoics believed that it was foolish not only to blame others, but to blame oneself when things do not turn out the way you wished. Use the space below to forgive yourself for something that you blamed yourself for in the past.

SMALL-MINDED PEOPLE BLAME OTHERS. AVERAGE PEOPLE BLAME THEMSELVES. THE WISE SEE ALL BLAME AS FOOLISHNESS.

EPICTETUS

Have you noticed the connection between your more disciplined mind and your mood? When you control your thoughts and feelings, how does it affect your outlook on life?

THE SOUL IS DYED THE COLOR OF ITS THOUGHTS. THINK ONLY ON THOSE THINGS THAT ARE IN LINE WITH YOUR PRINCIPLES AND CAN BEAR THE LIGHT OF DAY. THE CONTENT OF YOUR CHARACTER IS YOUR CHOICE. DAY BY DAY, WHAT YOU DO IS WHO YOU BECOME. YOUR INTEGRITY IS YOUR DESTINY - IT IS THE LIGHT THAT GUIDES YOUR WAY.

HERACLITUS

The Stoics believed that our actions are more important than our words. We can spout off about what we know or believe, but demonstrating it through our actions is what really matters. Can you think of a time you wished you had talked less and acted more? Use the space below to reflect.

THESE ARE THE SIGNS OF A WISE MAN: TO REPROVE NOBODY, TO PRAISE NOBODY, TO BLAME NOBODY, NOR EVEN SPEAK OF HIMSELF OR HIS OWN MERITS.

EPICTETUS

What are you doing to expand your mind on a regular basis?

THE MORE A MIND TAKES IN, THE MORE IT EXPANDS.

SENECA

STOIC SPOTLIGHT

CHRYSIPPUS

CHRYSIPPUS was born around 279 BCE in Cilicia in what is now Turkey. He moved to Athens when he was young and began studying with Cleanthes at the Stoic School.

Chrysippus developed the concept of propositional logic; that is, the idea that a statement can be true or false, but it can't be both. He helped advance the importance of living in accordance with nature and cultivating virtue as the key to eudaimonia, or flourishing. He believed that happiness and tranquility could be attained through the practice of virtue and the acceptance of fate.

Chrysippus also furthered the idea of Stoic physics, the branch of Stoicism that seeks to understand the way the universe works. He also developed a theory of determinism; that is, the idea that all events are determined by the laws of nature.

Although it's believed that he wrote over 700 books, much of Chrysippus's writing has been lost to time, with only a few passages remaining.

WISE PEOPLE ARE IN WANT OF NOTHING, AND YET NEED MANY THINGS. ON THE OTHER HAND, NOTHING IS NEEDED BY FOOLS, FOR THEY DO NOT UNDERSTAND HOW TO USE ANYTHING, BUT ARE IN WANT OF EVERYTHING.

CHRYSIPPUS

BE CONTENT

ACCEPTANCE AND contentment go hand in hand. When we accept what we can't control, we look inward for what we can. When we develop the skills to control our responses, we are on our way to contentment. Reducing our desire or cravings for things that we don't or can't have is another way to progress toward contentment.

In this section, we'll look at what the Stoics said about achieving contentment through the mastery of our own thoughts, feelings, and actions.

A GOOD CHARACTER IS THE ONLY GUARANTEE OF EVERLASTING, CAREFREE HAPPINESS. SENECA

Does your use of social media or other digital media contribute to a sense of FOMO, or fear of missing out? What steps have you taken, or can you now take, to reduce this source of negative emotions? What's stopping you from changing your relationship toward it?

What circumstances or people in your life are difficult for you to accept? What can you do to co-exist with the discomfort and achieve contentment?

HOW SATISFYING IT IS TO DISMISS AND BLOCK OUT ANY UPSETTING OR FOREIGN IMPRESSION, AND IMMEDIATELY TO HAVE PEACE IN ALL THINGS.

MARCUS AURELIUS

TRUE HAPPINESS IS TO ENJOY
THE PRESENT, WITHOUT
ANXIOUS DEPENDENCE UPON
THE FUTURE, NOT TO AMUSE
OURSELVES WITH EITHER HOPES
OR FEARS BUT TO REST SATISFIED
WITH WHAT WE HAVE, WHICH IS
SUFFICIENT, FOR HE THAT IS SO
WANTS NOTHING. THE GREATEST
BLESSINGS OF MANKIND ARE
WITHIN US AND WITHIN OUR
REACH. A WISE MAN IS CONTENT
WITH HIS LOT, WHATEVER IT
MAY BE, WITHOUT WISHING FOR
WHAT HE HAS NOT.

SENECA

Being content in the moment doesn't mean forgetting about the future entirely. How do you balance your present pleasures with your journey toward living a more virtuous life?

ENJOY PRESENT PLEASURES IN SUCH A WAY AS NOT TO INJURE FUTURE ONES.

SENECA

Contentment can't be achieved unless we stop comparing ourselves to others, but it can be hard to do. One of the emotions that must be mastered is that of coveting what others have. How can you gain control of this emotion?

HOW MUCH TIME HE GAINS WHO DOES NOT LOOK TO SEE WHAT HIS NEIGHBOR SAYS OR DOES OR THINKS, BUT ONLY AT WHAT HE DOES HIMSELF, TO MAKE IT JUST AND HOLY.

MARCUS AURELIUS

What do you need to be happy and content? Use the space below to write it down.

REMEMBER THAT VERY LITTLE IS NEEDED To MAKE A HAPPY LIFE.

MARCUS AURELIUS

ATTACH YOURSELF TO WHAT IS SPIRITUALLY SUPERIOR, REGARDLESS OF WHAT OTHER PEOPLE THINK OR DO. HOLD TO YOUR TRUE ASPIRATIONS NO MATTER WHAT IS GOING ON AROUND YOU.

EPICTETUS

How can you free yourself from the expectations of others so that you can live a life that is virtuous and dutiful, but free?

IS FREEDOM ANYTHING ELSE THAN THE RIGHT TO LIVE AS WE WISH? NOTHING ELSE.

EPICTETUS

REMEMBER THAT YOU MUST BEHAVE IN LIFE AS AT A DINNER PARTY. IS ANYTHING BROUGHT AROUND TO YOU? PUT OUT YOUR HAND AND TAKE YOUR SHARE WITH MODERATION. DOES IT PASS BY YOU? DON'T STOP IT. IS IT NOT YET COME? DON'T STRETCH YOUR DESIRE TOWARDS IT, BUT WAIT TILL IT REACHES YOU. DO THIS WITH REGARD TO CHILDREN, TO A WIFE, TO PUBLIC POSTS, TO RICHES, AND YOU WILL EVENTUALLY BE A WORTHY PARTNER OF THE FEASTS OF THE GODS. AND IF YOU DON'T EVEN TAKE THE THINGS WHICH ARE SET BEFORE YOU, BUT ARE ABLE EVEN TO REJECT THEM, THEN YOU WILL NOT ONLY BE A PARTNER AT THE FEASTS OF THE GODS, BUT ALSO OF THEIR EMPIRE.

EPICTETUS

Examine what you do in your life "for show" or to impress others. Is it the way you dress, the home you live in or something else? What would happen if you let go of this desire to impress and focused instead on what you need to make yourself happy? How would things be different?

FORTIFY YOURSELF WITH CONTENTMENT. IT IS AN IMPREGNABLE FORTRESS.

EPICTETUS

What do you have now that you once craved in the past? How can you learn to be satisfied with it instead of constantly wanting more?

DON'T DREAM ABOUT THINGS YOU DON'T HAVE. INSTEAD, THINK ABOUT THE BEST THINGS YOU NOW HAVE AND HOW MUCH YOU WOULD CRAVE THEM IF YOU DIDN'T HAVE THEM.

MARCUS AURELIUS

Instead of always trying to acquire more and different things, Stoicism encourages us to be content with what we have. How can you change your mindset so that what you have now is exactly enough?

The quote from Seneca below could be translated into modern speech as "the grass is always greener on the other side." This is something we know instinctively, but often ignore. Think about a time when you fell into the trap of thinking the grass was greener elsewhere. What did you learn from the experience?

FIX A LIMIT WHICH YOU WILL NOT EVEN DESIRE TO PASS, SHOULD YOU HAVE THE POWER. AT LAST, THEN, AWAY WITH ALL THESE TREACHEROUS GOODS! THEY LOOK BETTER TO THOSE WHO HOPE FOR THEM THAN TO THOSE WHO HAVE ATTAINED THEM. IF THERE WERE ANYTHING SUBSTANTIAL IN THEM, THEY WOULD SOONER OR LATER SATISFY YOU; AS IT IS, THEY MERELY ROUSE THE DRINKERS' THIRST.

SENECA

MICHEL DE MONTAIGNE

WHEN WoRKS OF THE classical world were revived during the Renaissance, philosophers began to rediscover the Stoics. One of them was French philosopher Michel Eyquem de Montaigne, born in 1533 to a wealthy family in Saint-Michel-de-Montaigne, France. He studied Latin and Greek as a child and law as an adult. He served as a local magistrate in the Bordeaux region and advised King Charles IX.

Montaigne's most famous work is *Essais* (Essays), published in 1580. The essays explored friendship, education, ethics, morality, and the human condition. They are considered the first examples of essay as a literary form. Montaigne was a pioneer in skepticism. He was influenced by the Stoics and admired them, but also critiqued them. He believed in the value of controlling one's own thoughts and emotions, and in relinquishing control over all else. But because he was a skeptic, he questioned the Stoic emphasis on wisdom and rationality. He wrote: "What Stoics did from virtue, I teach myself to do from temperament."

THE VALUE OF LIFE LIES NOT IN THE LENGTH OF DAYS, BUT IN THE USE WE MAKE OF THEM... WHETHER YOU FIND SATISFACTION IN LIFE DEPENDS NOT ON YOUR TALE OF YEARS, BUT ON YOUR WILL.

MICHEL DE MONTAIGNE

BE RESPONSIBLE TO OTHERS

WHILE SO MUCH of Stoicism is about centering on and developing the self, virtuous thoughts are not enough. To achieve a well-lived life, it's also important to take virtuous actions. Many of the Stoic philosophers stressed the importance of promoting the common good and doing our civic duty. By serving others, we can achieve the four aspects of virtue: courage, justice, wisdom, and temperance.

In this section, we'll look at how you can translate your virtuous thoughts into action.

I AM A CITIZEN OF THE WORLD.

EPICTETUS

IT IS OF COURSE REQUIRED OF A MAN THAT HE SHOULD BENEFIT HIS FELLOW-MEN—MANY IF HE CAN; IF NOT, A FEW; IF NOT A FEW, THOSE WHO ARE NEAREST; IF NOT THESE, HIMSELF. FOR WHEN HE RENDERS HIMSELF USEFUL TO OTHERS, HE ENGAGES IN PUBLIC AFFAIRS.

SENECA

What sense of responsibility do you have toward others in your community? To the world? How do you translate that into action?

WHEN MEN CHOOSE TO DO NOTHING, THEY ALSO LEARN TO DO EVIL.

CATO THE YOUNGER

WHENEVER YOU HAVE TROUBLE GETTING UP IN THE MORNING, REMIND YOURSELF THAT YOU'VE BEEN MADE BY NATURE FOR THE PURPOSE OF WORKING WITH OTHERS, WHEREAS EVEN UNTHINKING ANIMALS SHARE SLEEPING. AND IT'S OUR OWN NATURAL PURPOSE THAT IS MORE FITTING AND MORE SATISFYING.

MARCUS AURELIUS

How do you seek justice in the world while maintaining your Stoic virtues?

OFTEN INJUSTICE LIES IN WHAT YOU AREN'T DOING, NOT ONLY IN WHAT YOU ARE DOING.

MARCUS AURELIUS

The Stoics believed that we must be intentional about our duty to others; that it shouldn't be an afterthought. Think of your own character and virtue: what do you have to offer others? How can you intentionally offer it?

EVERY SOUL, THE PHILOSOPHER SAYS, IS INVOLUNTARILY DEPRIVED OF TRUTH; CONSEQUENTLY IN THE SAME WAY IT IS DEPRIVED OF JUSTICE AND TEMPERANCE AND BENEVOLENCE AND EVERYTHING OF THE KIND. IT IS MOST NECESSARY TO KEEP THIS IN MIND, FOR THUS THOU WILT BE MORE GENTLE TOWARDS ALL.

MARCUS AURELIUS

Stoicism encourages us to be humble. But that doesn't mean insignificant. What do you think you can do to make a significant contribution to the world?

How does service for others allow you to build and demonstrate your character?

WHATEVER ANYONE DOES OR SAYS, FOR MY PART I'M BOUND TO THE GOOD. IN THE SAME WAY AN EMERALD OR GOLD OR PURPLE MIGHT ALWAYS PROCLAIM: 'WHATEVER ANYONE DOES OR SAYS, I MUST BE WHAT I AM AND SHOW MY TRUE COLORS.'

MARCUS AURELIUS

REMIND YOURSELF
OF YOUR DUTY TO BE
A GOOD MAN AND
REHEARSE WHAT MAN'S
NATURE DEMANDS...
ALWAYS, THOUGH, IN
KINDNESS, INTEGRITY,
AND SINCERITY.

MARCUS AURELIUS

What do you believe is your life's purpose?

EVERYTHING, A HORSE, A VINE, IS CREATED FOR SoME DUTY. FOR WHAT TASK, THEN, WERE YoU YoURSELF CREATED? A MAN'S TRUE DELIGHT IS To DO THE THINGS HE WAS MADE FOR.

MARCUS AURELIUS

Commit yourself to at least three acts of service this month. After you have offered yourself in service, how did you feel? Use the space below to reflect on how serving others without any intent for personal gain helped you on your path toward a virtuous life.

Ultimately, the Stoics believed that we have a duty to both ourselves and to others to be the best person we can be. Use this space to commit to writing your vision of the best version of yourself that you can be in this world.

NOW IS THE TIME TO GET SERIOUS ABOUT LIVING YOUR IDEALS. HOW LONG CAN YOU AFFORD TO PUT OFF WHO YOU REALLY WANT TO BE? YOUR NOBLER SELF CANNOT WAIT ANY LONGER. PUT YOUR PRINCIPLES INTO PRACTICE–NOW. STOP THE EXCUSES AND THE PROCRASTINATION. THIS IS YOUR LIFE! YOU AREN'T A CHILD ANYMORE. THE SOONER YOU SET YOURSELF TO YOUR SPIRITUAL PROGRAM, THE HAPPIER YOU WILL BE. THE LONGER YOU WAIT, THE MORE YOU'LL BE VULNERABLE TO MEDIOCRITY AND FEEL FILLED WITH SHAME AND REGRET, BECAUSE YOU KNOW YOU ARE CAPABLE OF BETTER. FROM THIS INSTANT ON, VOW TO STOP DISAPPOINTING YOURSELF. SEPARATE YOURSELF FROM THE MOB. DECIDE TO BE EXTRAORDINARY AND DO WHAT YOU NEED TO DO–NOW.

EPICTETUS